A
Pathway
through the
Seasons
Written and Illustrated
by
Rose Blakeley

Copyright © 2008 Rose Blakeley

Published by Attitude Publishing

All rights reserved.

No part of this publication may be reproduced, stored in a retrieval system, or transmitted, in any form or by any means, electronic, mechanical, photocopying, recording or otherwise, without the prior permission of Attitude Publishing.

First Edition Printed March 2008

A record of this publication is available from the British Library

Email: garryblakeley@aol.com
www.apathwaythroughtheseasons.co.uk

Dedication

This book is dedicated
to my parents
John and Dr. Pamela Kendall
who opened my eyes to the magic of the seasons
with the gift of a wonderful childhood,
full of dreams and imagination.

Acknowledgements

I would like to thank the following for all their help and support:
Garry Blakeley, Sarah Kendall, Eddy Blakeley,
Jane Downes, Geoff Hutchinson, Terry Hulf,
Susan Benyounes, Darren Trevette
and all my family and friends for their
continuous interest and encouragement.

Contents

Jack Frost
The Windy Day
A Monster from the Sea
The Scarecrow
Evening Flight
The Ceremony of May
The Giants' Parade
Wayland's Smithy
The Green Man
Robin-in-the-Hood
Solstice at the Long Man
Call of the Fairies
Chittlebirch
Harvest Home
The Gypsies' Tale
Waiting for the Moon
The Fall of a Saxon King
The Pathway of Old
Bonfire on the Battlefield
The Coming of Christmas

Jack Frost

When the world was sleeping in cocoons of blanket fold,
I went out a-walking through the mist and cutting cold.
So early was that day, the sky was pale, just as a pearl
And in the waking of that morning, then, a New Year did unfurl.
 The weathercock he shivered and turned his tail into the breeze,
As the echoes of the wassail songs ran round and round the apple trees.
 The yellow-grey sun blinked, but it had neither glare nor gleam,
Then, something moved before my eyes, it was as though I was in a dream!

 That dawn I saw a little one having a time so fine,
Swinging on the ivy rope and sliding down the holly spine.
The mistletoe he sparkled and frosted the rosehip red,
He dusted diamonds upon the grass and the last of autumn's shed.
 Each windowpane he clouded obscuring the garden's view,
Then, on the path he merrily danced with neither shirt nor shoe,
For all he wore was the finest mesh, like the wings of a damselfly
And the cloth that ran along his legs was of the brightest pea-green dye.

 His tinted hair it sprouted and was fashioned here and there,
Whilst an array of icy stars, like jewels, shone in the ivory air,
And as he skipped over the borders, now of a sepia, frozen ground,
So light was he upon his toes he didn't make a sound.
 So with fingers, long and thin, he spun the last of his winter's lace,
And back he looked upon his work, from a smiling, shimmering face.
 Then at last, when his task it was complete, it was time for him to flee,
Leaving his creation of crystal charm, a magical world for all to see!

The Windy Day

    High upon the Parlour, where the ladies they once strolled,
I am embraced by the winter with its presence here so bold.
The wind it stings my face, for the rain is tipped with ice
And my long, red hair a-flowing, through roughly it does slice.
    The faint and mottled sky frames an outline carved of stone,
A fortress still and fallen, which guards the coastline from its throne,
For it watches over the ocean and those upon it each who sail-
The sailors of the sea who brave the dangers of a gale.
    A sun, small and pale, peeps from a moody peach-pink light,
Whilst swooping seagulls cackle, rejoicing in the gift of flight.
Along the beach they glide to a harbour bleak and grave,
Just as its arm is swallowed, whole, by a huge crashing wave…
    I watch it explode into clouds of froth, tinted blue and grey, in awe,
As fishing boats they huddle and seem to shiver upon the shore,
Before the freezing water, which fringes the sleepy town of old,
Where the pewter streets are empty as folk shelter from the cold.
    But lights show signs of comfort as the open fires are lit
And around the worn, oak tables gatherings of people sit,
Indulging in the fine ale in a cosy, beamed back-bar,
Oblivious to the elements, now a long way away by far!
    A session unfolds as instruments entwine, the evening will be long,
Whilst in the breeze, the pub sign swings, singing its rusty song.

A Monster from the Sea

As the wild winds wail from the ocean, lost am I to the window's view,
For like a phantom's haunting howl, the sash it squeezes through,
Whilst rearing high, into a rampant spray, the sea smashes into the bay,
And like an orchestra driven to madness, nature's in chaos this cheerless day.

Against a sky just fit to burst, the naked branches of winter clash,
Then, sweeping sheets of needled-rain begin to batter and to lash-
A monster made of cloud! I watch the storm now make its course,
Beating the gardens down below with frightful, formidable force.

The autumn's twisted leaves toss and tumble across the grass,
And over a scattering of snowdrops then, in their spiralled shapes they pass.
Pale, delicate flowers with those crinkled grins of green,
Like lanterns they hold their heads high, so in the gloom can still be seen.

From the darkness of the heavens explodes a brilliant and electric light,
This dragon is breathing lightening spears and throwing them down with all its might,
And too, the armies of thunder march, onto a ferocious battle they go,
Over a leaden, luminous horizon with a flickering, unnatural glow…

The sea winds chase the depression beyond, with their breath consistent and cold,
Then, they part the battered canopy above, revealing tiny pockets of gold,
And as evening sunshine at last breaks through, way above the herring gulls soar,
Whilst below, a calmness soothes the world, and peace is here once more!.

The Scarecrow

   Out in all weathers
But he doesn't make a sound,
Fastened to a piece of wood
The scarecrow can be found.
  His pumpkin-head thinks not,
But I'm sure I saw him move
And the fact that he winked at me
Is nothing I could prove!

  Crows tug at his rag-patched clothes,
They never seem to scare,
But the farmer does not worry
Although his fields are bare.
  Now I see him watch the sunset,
The celandine and violet, his array-
But I'm sure that this morning
He was facing the other way!

Evening Flight

"How strange the world seems from up-side-down",
Said a sleepy voice beneath a leathery gown,
"Come on, let's go and greet the night,
We'll leave the barn and practice flight!"…

So the two of them left their haven high
To explore the realms of an endless sky,
Over the shadowed farmyard they did go
And the rippled rooftop of the house below.
The cattle-track they traced, across the fields it did coil,
Fragrant was the air from the warm, open soil,
For spring had awakened and that very evening set free,
And soon the leafless landscape in full bloom it would be!
Onto the old, gnarled woods, then, of oak, they did fly,
Over its twisted silhouette, its braided branches held high,
And to chase the verdant banks of the lanes they were keen,
As wild arum hoods unfolded into a fresh, fluorescent green,
Amidst pure, white wind-flowers with a gilded glow,
Kissed by a full, mustard moon rising on the horizon low.
The face of dusk deepened from a pale indigo-blue,
With a scattering of stars, into an ebony hue.
Then, out of its darkness and into the breeze,
Two travellers danced joyfully beyond the trees,
With bodies of fur, wings jagged and bare,
They had keys to the eternal kingdom of air!

When dawn peeped over the horizon pale,
They returned to their home, but with many a tale…
Back over the fields, and the yard of the farm,
To the barn they did go, to sleep safe from harm.

The Ceremony of May

   Darkness fades before a new moon, a crescent pale and still,
A gathering awaits dawn's magic, figures silhouette the hill.
   The lime leaf is entwined with the hawthorn's pure, white lace,
Whilst flowers bloom within ivy crowns around each bonny face.
   From garlands in the early mist, coloured ribbons fly,
As the top hat, garnished with feather and oak, on each head is held high.
   Now, the sky it blushes crimson, so the dancers greet the sun,
Hand-in-hand with time once more, May's morning has begun…

   An extraordinary assembly fills the town of Hastings old,
A fusion of costumes, wonderful and bright, a vision to behold!
   We join in celebration by the shores of a golden sea,
As from the cheers, at last, once more, the Jack-in-the-Green is free!
   All is still, and a silence falls from the chanting of his name,
Then, the ladies dance, with charm and grace, around his fabulous frame,
And down come the petals thrown from each and every sleeve,
Towards the winding, narrow streets the procession now does weave.

   Leaping and prancing, the mystical mass it moves with spectacular flare,
Frolicking and flaunting with hankies a-flying over antler, horn and hair.
The clacking of sticks and the chinking of bells, compete with the cry of the crowds,
Then, passes the wondrous parade of giants, with their heads up in the clouds.
   The playful wind is warm and under a canopy of blue,
Good entertainment merges with the finest of nature's brew,
Whilst the hobbyhorse he teases, as each painted face does glow,
Then, after the maypole ritual, up to the castle they must go.

   At last, we wait with baited breath, for Jack to leave his stand,
The seasons have turned full circle as we watch the merry band.
Guarded closely he faces his fate, the minstrels tune the drum,
Round and round the leaf-men go, for the 'One-in-the-Green' his time has come!
   With the traditional, token clashing of wood, the enchantment takes its hold
And we cast away the memories of a winter long and cold.
   So sadly Jack, now, you must fall… and down he lies for all to see!
He's slain now! Strip his coat and keep. The spirit of summer at last is free!

The Giants' Parade

As the fishing boats rest, to sail now no more,
There's an awakening here at old Rock-a-Nore,
For the spirit of Beltane is wild and has life,
And in this theatrical display of folk it is rife.

As they pass the net shops, tall and dark,
Each striking personality makes its mark,
But on only one image, is my full gaze now set,
As I see a parade I will never forget…

Unaware of all else, a low drum beat calls,
Then slowly upon me a deep shadow falls,
I turn and gaze up to an inquisitive eye,
From an ageless face framed by a blue sky.

Towering above dancers, music and song,
He marches with grace although heavy and strong,
Others now follow and in wonder I look
At a collection of characters as though from a book.

From garlands of green, to raven-winged hair,
Strange skin of silver, to a witch's stare,
Black cats may 'fly' from The Stag, so beware!
A strong spell of magic is loose in the air.

With leaf-men and Morris the great giants play,
Shrouded with mystery, they now make their way
To the final slopes up where they'll stand and be still,
Till the new light of summer will shine on the hill!

Wayland's Smithy

Across the downs a white horse rides,
A galloping outline, its form curves and slides,
It imagines a pathway stretching miles beyond view,
The route of the Ridgeway chasing an horizon of blue.
 And also, before me, this ancient landscape strides,
To a special place, which under a beech grove hides,
A circle of stones around an oval mound,
Where our ancestors rest in a chamber below ground.
But this monument is guarded by a figure of old-
By a Saxon god with many a story told…
 Wayland, the smith, one of mystery,
Within the lime tree and bluebell his spirit is free,
For his art holds magic to this day still,
It's here in the wind, which blows beyond to the hill.
 Now, if you should pass upon a horse with no shoe,
Weary from travel and you know not what to do,
Leave your steed at the mound alone for a while,
With a silver coin, and on your return you surely will smile,
For re-shod your horse now it will be
And your silver coin gone, but no sign of he!

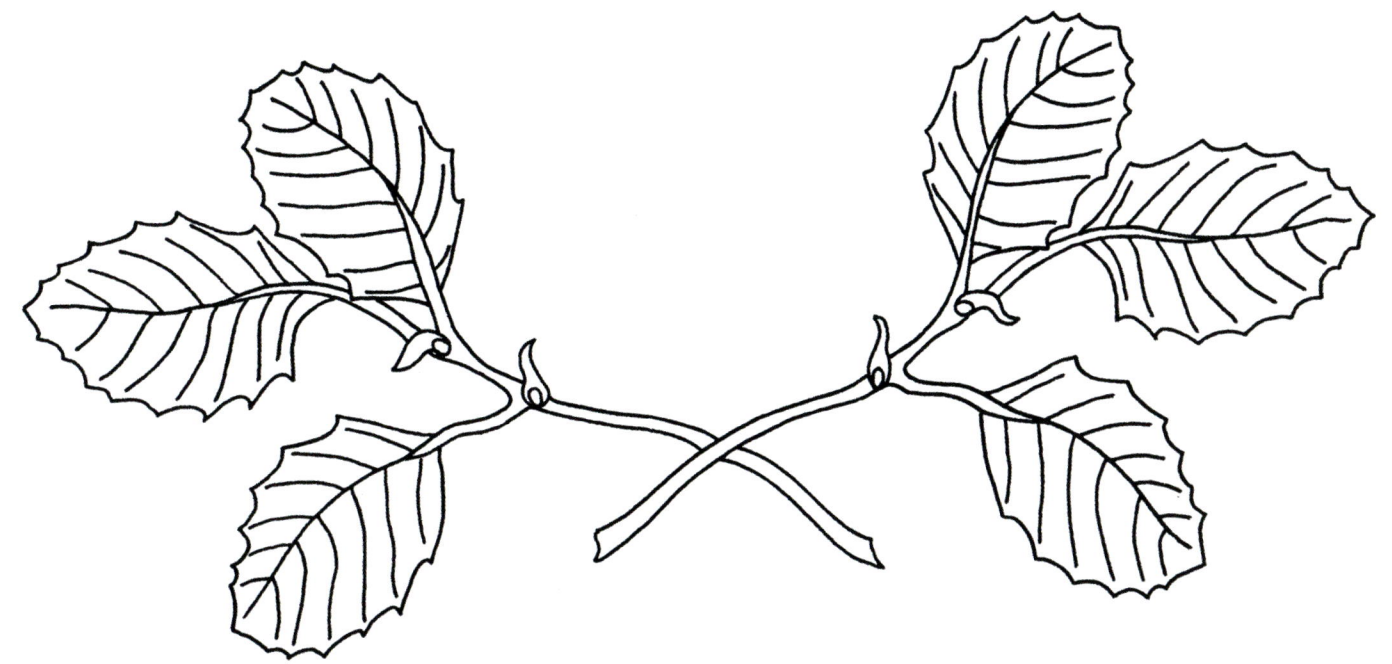

Now, if ever to Berkshire shall I return?
This hidden place to revisit, I shall yearn,
To walk around the circle, a rosette of stone,
And I'll wonder if I shall be there alone!

The Green Man

"Step into the forest, warm and bright,
Drink from the cup of golden light,
And deep within you, your instincts will glow,
Whilst through your body, the sweet winds will blow.
 Look up to my wild and mottled face,
Where foliage and flowers softly enlace."

…I wonder, to me, now, what will befall?
As I stand here alone, I, one so small,
But I hear your words, as the great boughs sway-
Then, in your emerald arms I gently lay.
 Shafts of sun flood through new lime leaves,
Which shimmer and dance as the treetop heaves
And the air is dense with blossom's scent,
All beings living are quiet and content.
 Moved and moulded by this mysterious hold,
I am taken and enlightened by an energy of old.
Its music drifts sweetly, through a pale haze of blue,
And its notes are a calling for the chosen few…

"The wonder of the forest is an untamed dream,
And nature has taken you into its realm.
You are free now from the world you know,
Feel me as the very seasons grow.
 Now, you can fly into a world serene,
Never lose touch with my spirit of green!"

Robin-in-the-Hood

    Long, long ago in the deep mists of time,
There once was a village, and Loxley was its name.
    Then, from out of the darkness, one night the soldiers came,
The houses they were burnt and its people they were slain.
    But, there was a man called Ailric, with his son away rode free,
For guardian of a sacred arrow, a silver arrow, was he.
To the miller went his boy, whilst the sheriff a trap did lay-
A trap to steal the arrow… Ailric lost his life that dreadful day!

    Later on, by many years, from that boy, a man he became,
Young and strong and free was he. Robin was his name.
    One-day the king's deer he did kill, but that deer he was not to keep,
For Guy of Gisburne caught him and threw him into the dungeons deep.
    There he met Will Scarlet; they escaped with others, and a plan,
But trapped was Robin at the castle gate, so up the stairs he ran.
Up the stairs ran he, up and through a wooden door
And the Lady Marion there he met. Her beauty never had he seen before.

    "You're like a morning of the May!" to her he softly said,
He placed a hood, then, over his head and through the window fled,
Into the depths of Sherwood, into the forest of the green,
To join his friends around the fire, not to be found, nor to been seen.
    In the haze of that evening light, a vision he did see…
    A man, crowned with a stag's head! "I am Herne the hunter!" then, said he.
"You are the chosen one, to help the poor. This is your destiny.
You are their hope", he said, "Robin-in-the-hood. So must it be!"

    The calling of fate he followed, the time was near, it could be seen,
For the powers of light and darkness, with him had always been.
It was time to fight injustice, now his kingdom he would claim,
And claim would he a Wayland sword. Albion was its name!
Then, once his bow, it had been strung, with Herne he would be strong,
So, returned he to the forest to be joined by Little John,
Much, the miller's son, and Friar Tuck - the size of ten!
    The time to fight had just begun, for this band of merry men.

    One-day, the sheriff he gave news of a contest for one and all,
Of archery held at Nottingham within the castle wall.
The hooded-man would come, he hoped, the silver arrow being the prize,
And the hooded-man must go, to win, but as an outlaw in disguise…
    The contest it was won that day by Robin-in-the-hood,
So he took the prize, the sacred arrow, and fled deep into the wood.
    Then, the Lady Marion declared her love, to Robin, for all to see,
So they were wed, by Herne, amongst the trees, and blessed they would be!

Solstice at the Long Man

    Today I walk the South Downs Way
With my childhood hand-in-hand,
For memories through my mind do sway
Of those summers long ago.
And still, the bright flowers adorn the grass,
The daisy and buttercup bold,
Which pave the pathway as I pass,
With the tiny speedwell swaddled.

    The exquisite orchid quietly speckles
The slopes and shady banks,
A delicate purple with crimson freckles,
Scattered sparsely below butterflies of blue.
    Skippers dither with the marbled white
And the joyful fritillary,
Whilst a dragonfly swoops with all his might
As busy bees tumble and hum.

    High above, a twittering lark
Celebrates the gift of flight,
With an explosion of song he makes his mark,
Below a scorching sun.
    The horizon it runs to a distant sea,
Kissed by a cloudless sky
And eternity's landscape is given to me
From the Ridgeway's endless track.

    And so upon this solstice day
The chalk giant guards the hill,
From his verdurous slope along the Way
Above the corn and poppy red.
And now I watch the blushed sun splash
My view with dusk's bright splendour,
As chattering swifts, they chase and dash
Up into the evening wind.

Call of the Fairies

   Colours deepen as darkness falls,
Revealing the face of dusk,
And the flame of sundown quietly crawls
Across a cloudless sky.
   The scented wind it washes
My mind beyond it all,
As the garden slowly hushes,
Except for a cricket's evening song.

   Then I hear a sound, which leads me to
The shadows beyond the borders,
Up the steps and quietly through
The flowers, which smell like honeydew.
   A periwinkle with its winding trail
Through the purple viola weaves,
Whilst giving shelter to a snoozing snail
Below lemon marguerites.

   The moths embrace the cooling air
Above the fig tree's waxen palms,
And bindweed blooms twist, like parasols fair
As they close in the fading light.
   Roses cloak the sloping walls,
Blushing pink, with ivory eyes,
Their petals drape softly over ivy falls
Below a bright half moon.

   Now, surrounded am I, by the stirring of leaves
And a moving of tiny lights,
There's a whispering in the great old trees-
Magic all around!
   Soon, it is time for me to leave
For the fairies will come to dance,
To the lively tune of Midsummer's Eve,
But when no one in the garden is to be seen!

Chittlebirch

The cool, dark pond lies below the trees
And moves only for the lily in a warm July breeze,
Whilst dancing mosquito pirouette in full flight
And in their mass entertain me in the rays of sunlight.
 A dragonfly swoops in a blaze of bright green,
Then hovers before me in its magnificent sheen.
I blow the 'clock' of the dandelion high
As the swallows, I watch, dive down from the sky
To scoop gnats from the grasses and the daisy white,
Then up, and above, to the clouds beyond sight.
 A neatly mown lawn greets a well-weeded bed
And across it a blaze of multicolour is spread,
Into a beautiful braid, the blooms they do bind
Below a giant sunflower, radiant and refined.
 The wind is so warm and brings sleep to my eye
As into its fragrance I release a small sigh,
No words for its wonder, its perfume is strong-
In this enchanting garden I shall always belong!
 Away from the orchard, secret pathways unfold,
Then, before me a house stands! It is strong, proud and old.
This house it has carried me my whole childhood through,
And cradled me gently as the wild, winter winds blew.
I gaze up at its windows and terracotta walls,
Its crooked back door, where the geranium flower falls…
 The melody of memory remains deep in my heart
And from the bond of a family I never shall part,
Wherever I settle, wherever I roam,
Chittlebirch will always be a place that I call home!

Harvest Home

    The crown of the year is here once more!
The tinhorn was blown at dawn,
For blown it was at the farmhouse door
As to the fields the reapers did go.
   Worked they all day till the sun did wane,
Then the sickles were thrown in as one,
To sever the very last of that which did remain
So the 'corn spirit' could blame no one man.
   After 'crying the neck' and with the last of the stalk,
The dolly of gold then was crafted,
Amongst flowers and leaf, home-bound now they walk,
All now walk with her long ribbons a-flowing.

   Alight now are the home fires bright,
Whilst garlands hang high and hang low,
To the supper of the harvest, they come now this night,
To the harvest they all gaily come.
   For slain is the fattened farmyard beast,
The hare hunted and the bird of game,
And brought to the great barn for the fabulous feast,
With warm bread and fresh fruit puddings.
   Jigs and reels, lively the fiddler will play
Amidst toasting with ale and cider,
And dance, dance will they, till the early light of day,
Till the gilded sun will awaken.

   But when the feasting is all done
And have faded the home fires bright,
When all the songs from flushed faces are sung
And the flagons are empty and dry,
On a special chair then, the dolly shall lay,
Once given her final plait,
And to the parlour carried where she will stay
As guardian of the next harvest…
   The crown of the year was here once more!
The tinhorn was blown at dawn,
For blown it was at the farmhouse door
As to the fields the reapers did go.

The Gypsies' Tale

Freedom it flowed their very veins through,
And where they would settle, no one knew,
For they travelled and drifted like a restless wind,
A long road winding for all destined.

With horse to wagon, round the big wheels rolled,
Around to the sound of stories retold
And no worries had they, but where to stop, to be still,
To brew tea and cook up a warm filling meal.

Now, in the dew-drenched mornings the families all,
Mother and father and children small,
To the fields of Kent and Sussex went they
To pick the hop each glorious day.

So faces of bronze chased a sun still high,
Whilst the last jewels of the meadow reached up to the sky-
The pimpernel scarlet, with its weather foretold,
And white mayweeds tangled with the corn marigold.

   Then at nightfall, when all the work was done,
After 'hopping-pot stew', so begun the fun…
  Merry music, dancing and ballads sung,
Each passed down from the elders to the young.

  Passion was potent, and below many a moon
Was a gypsy kiss stolen to a slow fiddle tune,
For evenings spent round the campfires were long
And to each other these travellers would always belong.

Waiting for the Moon

    The flaxen fields, now sleeping, sigh softly as I gaze,
Ignited by a scarlet sun, which on the horizon low does laze.
My view beyond glows auburn, it is silent now and still,
Its only movement is a leaping hare racing across the hill-
Across the slopes it prances and passes the standing stones,
Then vanishes, as if by magic, as the cool wind gently moans.
   Slowly the mist is gathering below the embers of the sky,
The air is damp and filled with smoke from a woodman's fire close by.

    The shadows of the brimstone trees lengthen as darkness falls,
And the silence only broken, as a swooping barn owl calls.
I watch the odd leaf flee, then to the ground it flutters down,
And adds another to the patchwork of early autumn's rainbow-gown.
    I walk with the dusk alone. I've been waiting so long to see,
So patiently I've been a-waiting for the moon to be set free…
   At last the time has come, for the sky once more is bright
And over the canopy of the forest is a rising, radiant light!

  A shining, luminous form I watch slowly now appear,
Then, loose at last, into a deepening blue as a perfect, saffron sphere.
Its beams are of a honey hue and tints the valley way below,
And then across the ancient burial mounds a shimmer it does throw.
    I find myself a-wandering, to maybe just get nearer,
To maybe touch its cheek, or maybe just to see it clearer.
But, beyond my reach it stays, so to the moon I say farewell,
And as I turn to leave, I know, that I'll be always under its spell!

The Fall of a Saxon King

The loosened leaf from the treetop flicks,
The year is ending of ten sixty-six.
Armies are marching from sea and land,
Now time holds history in an icy hand.
 The invaders are strong, their energy stored,
Greedy for war, loyal to their lords,
Mounted and armed, strong at the bow,
Superior in tactics, forward they go
Into a wall of shield, along the crest of the hill,
A tightly packed rank of strong, Saxon will,
Ready to die for country and king,
Armed with axes and primitive sling.
 So under the eyes of October skies,
The hills are filled with cold battle cries,
The endless clash of metal and man,
Slashing, slaughtering anyway they can…
 Then, William appears as a vision to all,
For his troops had feared that he did fall,
And now arrows are raining like deadly hail,
Whilst the Saxon forces become weak and frail,
And finally, before those, who see and take breath,
In moments, King Harold is hacked down to his death.
 The Golden Dragon of Wessex is lost,
And the men of the English have paid a great cost,
They died for their country, sword in hand,
But the blood and the spirit remain deep in the land,
And as the standard of victory, by the Duke has been won,
The Norman Conquest, this day, has begun!

The Pathway of Old

    Along the way of old I walk, towards the town of Rye,
Its stones blush cadmium-yellow as the sun commands the sky.
Its corners and bends I follow, I watch a drifting cloud or two,
Which sail like giant tall-ships an endless ocean through.
Before me the horizon beckons as I hear history passing by,
I imagine armies advancing, the echoes of battle cry.

    Then, lost am I to a whistling wind, one playful and so bold,
And in a flurry, the leaves up high it whisks in a blaze of rusted-gold.
    Now, the weather frowns upon me from a canopy of grey,
But the toadstools bright along the path guide me on my way,
And all along the ochre acorn upon the hedgerow shines,
As the rosehip and the berry of the bryony entwines.

    Now, autumn has grown weary, for its season it has turned,
And with winter's imminent arrival, its presence will be spurned.
Already the leaf he's stolen from each bough high and low,
And left the ruddy land, once green, alone to the cry of the crow!
    Oh what now of the mayflower? The daisy and buttercup bright?
Now, those lay deep within the soil, until the spring's new light.

    The fields are flushed deep crimson as each shadow softly falls,
And huddle the sheep upon the slopes as a faint fog slowly crawls,
But, it is the eve of Halloween, so to the pumpkin patch we'll go
And the Jack-o'-lantern will be made, then from the hearth he'll glow.
    Cold it grows, but along the coast the bonfires soon we'll see,
For power we give to a waning sun and from the darkness will be free!

Bonfire on the Battlefield

Remember, remember the fifth of November,
The gunpowder treason and plot.
I see no reason why gunpowder and treason
Should ever be forgot…

Darkness descends on a small town, guarded by the abbey wall,
It waits in anticipation, as across the moon the clouds do crawl,
But from every window shines a light, whilst house-parties begin within,
As the Guy stands stern upon The Green, soon to meet his gathering.
Now, one and all, they gradually greet the bar of the old King's Head,
And from pewter tankards overflowing, each and all are fed.
Costumes mingle from ages lost, with faces as black as the night,
Curiously painted and some with masks, a beast, or just full of fright!

The cold now bites, but the street at last is a mass of marching fire,
With each society's banner, held high, by members in their unique attire
And the procession passes with a wave of warmth from torches of tangerine blaze,
Accompanied by drumming and the fire-carts' roar, which then vanishes into a haze!
Yes, into a haze they vanish… but onto the battlefield reappear,
Surrounding the silent mound of wood, now filling it with fear,
Then, each torch is thrown, by one and all, the bonfire being their aim
And up it flares firing a fizzing of sparks from a dancing, flickering flame.

Up faces slant, as one by one the almighty fireworks explode,
Whizzing, hissing, cracking and banging, one by one they quickly unload
Up into the sky as serpents of gold, or rainbowed fountains of light
And with the inevitable eruption of an effigy, the horizon is a fabulous sight!
As the smoke it drifts across the field dividing people into shades of grey,
In my mind, I hear the whispers of time, the memories before this day
And I think of a year, of 1605 and how close Parliament came to fall,
In the echoes of time I hear it now, the chant sung by each one and all…

Holla boys, holla boys, let the bells ring.
Holla boys, holla boys, God save the king!

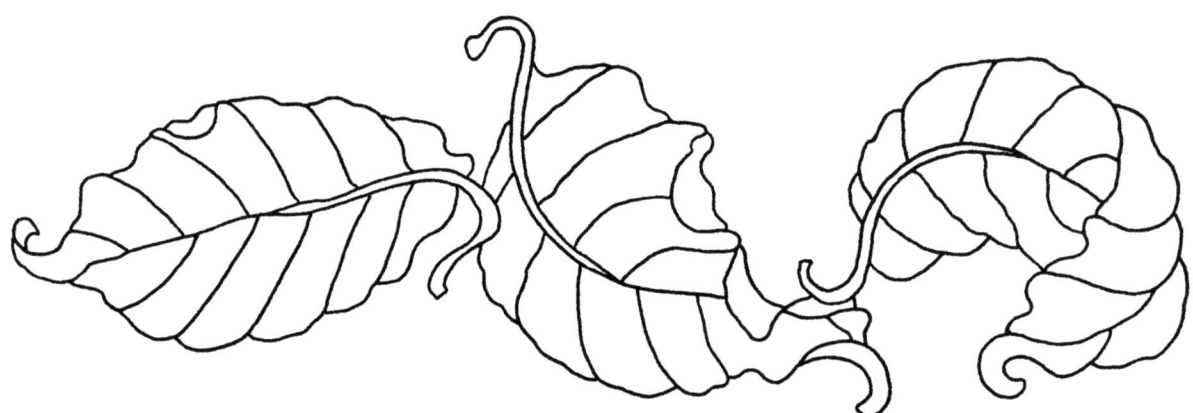

The Coming of Christmas

    The pure light of morning meets a landscape white with snow
And the winding stream, once busy, now into ice does flow,
On the horizon there is a lull, which under a blanket of grey does lie-
The only sounds are raucous rooks, flocking in the fields near by.

    Excited children peep through the frosted windowpane,
For to build a snowman in the garden, firstly is their aim,
Then, to gather all the evergreens and hang high the mistletoe,
So with the wicker basket creaking, a-collecting they do go.
   For a girl, the trailing ivy and for a boy, the holly leaf,
Studded with scarlet berries, they curve and twist into a wreath.
The farmhouse kitchen, then, they deck along the old, oak beam
And in the candlelight the horse brasses and copper saucepans gleam.
    The marbled moon retires from a freezing ink-blue sky,
As the North Star winks and twinkles as Christmas Eve draws nigh,
The Yule log has been kindled from the embers of the old
And the hearth is now an amber blaze to chase away the cold.
    There's the sweetest smell of pine from the shimmering, festive tree,
And on the table is the finest food, a feast for all to see-
Oranges and almonds, honey-ham and sugar mice,
Mince pies and chocolate truffles, hot punch with cider and spice.
    The singers greet the doorway with the mummers dressed to cheer,
And the resonant ring of the great church bells, then they gladly hear,
So with their lanterns a-swinging, to the village they all go,
As the windows of stained glass in the darkness brightly glow.

    The sweet notes of the carols steal the silence of this night,
Then softly, once more, the snowflakes fall, magical in their flight.
 Piles of parcels sparkle to the sound of a distant sleigh-
For passed has Father Christmas, bringing forth the joyous day!